FIRE TRUCKS

by Darlene R. Stille

Content Adviser: Jeff Sedivec, President,
California State Firefighters' Association
Reading Adviser: Dr. Linda D. Labbo,
Department of Reading Education, College of Education,
The University of Georgia

Compass Point Books
Minneapolis, Minnesota

Compass Point Books
3722 West 50th Street, #115
Minneapolis, MN 55410

Visit Compass Point Books on the Internet at *www.compasspointbooks.com* or e-mail your request to *custserv@compasspointbooks.com*

Photographs ©: Jim Regan/Dembinsky Photo Associates, cover, 16-17; U.S. Department of Agriculture, 1, 22; Dembinsky Photo Associates, 4-5, 12-13, 14-15; Unicorn Stock Photos/Andre Jenny, 6-7; John D. Cunningham/Visuals Unlimited, 8-9; Joseph A. Pinto/Dembinsky Photo Associates, 10-11, 24; Bob Krist/Corbis, 18; Unicorn Stock Photos/Novastock, 20-21; William B. Folsom, 26-27.

Editors: E. Russell Primm, Emily Dolbear, and Pam Rosenberg
Photo Researcher: Svetlana Zhurkina
Photo Selector: Linda S. Koutris
Designer: Melissa Voda

Library of Congress Cataloging-in-Publication Data
Stille, Darlene R.
    Fire trucks / by Darlene R. Stille.
        v. cm.— (Transportation / Darlene R. Stille)
    Includes bibliographical references and index.
    Contents: Where's the fire?—The fire engine—Old time fire engines—The ladder truck—The fire chief's car—Fire tanker trucks—Airport fire trucks—Rescue trucks—Clean-up trucks—Fire department ambulance—Communication units—Other fire "trucks".
    ISBN 0-7565-0288-8 (hardcover)
    1. Fire engines—Juvenile literature. [1. Fire engines.] I. Title.
    TH9372 .S75 2002
    628.9'25—dc21   2002002951

Table of Contents

Where's the Fire?

Let's look inside a fire station. We can see big, shiny fire trucks inside.

An alarm goes off. A fire is raging somewhere. The fire fighters jump into the fire trucks.

Sirens wail. Lights flash. Bells clang. The fire trucks are on the way.

The Fire Engine

The first truck that gets to the fire is the fire engine. A fire engine is also called a pumper. It carries big hoses.

Fire fighters hook up the hoses. One hose goes from the fire hydrant to the fire engine. A pump in the fire engine pushes water through other hoses. A motor makes the pump work. Fire fighters use the hoses to pour water on the fire.

Old-Time Fire Engines

The first fire engines were simple wooden tubs on wheels. People had to pump water from each tub to a hose by hand.

Later, fire engines had pumps that used steam. These fire engines burned coal or wood to make water so hot that it turned to steam. Black smoke and hot sparks flew out of the fire engine. Fire fighters or horses pulled the steam engine to a fire.

9

The Ladder Truck

The ladder truck carries long and short ladders. Fire fighters use ladders to reach windows or roofs and to rescue people from a fire.

Ladder trucks carry long hooks and other tools. Fire fighters use the tools to break windows and punch holes in roofs. They do this to let smoke out and to look for hidden fire. Ladder trucks are sometimes called hook-and-ladder trucks.

The Fire Chief's Car

The fire chief rides to the fire in a car or a small truck. The fire chief is sometimes called the commander.

The fire chief's car has special radios. These are used to talk to the fire fighters. If the fire is really big, the fire chief will use the radios to call for more fire trucks.

Fire Tanker Trucks

NO 425 FORD OWOSSO TWP. FIRE DEPT. SUPER TANKER

What if the fire is far away from a fire hydrant? What if a farmhouse catches fire? What if a field or a forest catches fire?

The fire fighters must bring lots of water with them. They bring the water in big tanks on special fire trucks. Pumps on the tanker trucks push water into the hoses.

Airport Fire Trucks

Airports have special fire trucks to fight airplane fires. Airport fire trucks look like other fire trucks, but they have special chemicals inside their tanks.

The chemicals make foam. Water will not stop airplane fuel from burning. Fire fighters must spray foam to put out airplane fires.

Rescue Trucks

Fire trucks are not always made for fighting fires. Some are made for rescuing people who are trapped.

Rescue trucks have no hoses or ladders. Rescue trucks carry special tools, though. One of these tools is called the "jaws of life." Fire fighters use these tools to free people from wrecked cars. They also use these tools to get people out of buildings that are falling down.

Clean-Up Trucks

Special fire trucks carry tools and chemicals to take care of dangerous spills. These trucks go to highway accidents. Fire fighters on these trucks clean up spilled gasoline.

These trucks go to train wrecks, too. Dangerous chemicals often spill out of wrecked railroad cars. The fire fighters clean up these leaks and spills, too.

Fire Department Ambulance

What if someone gets hurt? What if someone gets very sick? Call 911. The fire department ambulance will come to the rescue.

People called paramedics ride in the ambulance. They provide first aid. They put the sick or injured person in the ambulance. They rush to the nearest hospital.

Communication Units

Sometimes many fire trucks must go to a big fire. Someone must tell all the fire fighters what to do.

Trucks called command units or communication units go to big fires. Fire chiefs work in these trucks. They learn all about the fire. They tell groups of fire fighters how to put out the blaze.

Other Fire "Trucks"

Some fire "trucks" are not trucks at all. They are air- planes, helicopters, or boats.

Fire-fighting airplanes and helicopters fly over big forest fires. They dump water or chemicals on the flames.

Fireboats go to burning ships or docks. They pump water on the fire.

There are many kinds of fire trucks. Fire fighters use these trucks to rescue people from all kinds of dangers.

Glossary

injured—hurt

steam—water that has been heated to its boiling point

wrecked—broken or ruined

Did You Know?

Before fire engines, people formed "bucket brigades" to put out fires. First, people stood in a long line. Next, they filled buckets with water and passed them from one person to another. Then, the last person in line threw the water on the fire. Another long line of people passed the empty buckets back to be refilled.

Boston set up the first paid fire department in America in 1679.

Benjamin Franklin set up a volunteer fire department in Philadelphia in 1763. It was the first volunteer fire department in America.

Fire departments today work as hard to prevent fires as they do at putting out fires.

Two terrible fires broke out on October 8, 1871. That day, the Great Chicago Fire burned most of the city to the ground. About 250 people died. The town of Peshtigo, Wisconsin, also burned down. More than 1,110 people died in that fire.

Fire Prevention Week in the United States has been held every October since 1922.

Want to Know More?

At the Library

Bingham, Caroline. *Mighty Machines: Fire Truck.* New York: Dorling Kindersley, 2000.

Lippman, Peter. *Fire Engine No. 1.* New York: Workman, 2001.

Teitelbaum, Michael. *If I Could Drive a Fire Truck!* New York: Scholastic, 2001.

On the Web

Fire Administration Kids Page

http://www.usfa.fema.gov/kids/

For fire-safety information and games for kids as well as resources for parents and teachers

Risk Watch: Kids Only

http://www.nfpa.org/riskwatch/kids.html

For games that teach safety, including fire safety

Smokey Bear

http://www.smokeybear.com/

To play games as well as read information about how to prevent forest fires

Sparky the Fire Dog
http://www.sparky.org/index.html
For fire-safety information and a fire truck picture gallery

Through the Mail
United States Fire Administration
Publications Center
16825 South Seton Avenue
Emmitsburg, MD 21727
To write for information on fire prevention and safety

On the Road
The New York City Fire Museum
278 Spring Street
New York, NY 10013
To learn more about the history of fire fighting and the New York City Fire Department

Index

About the Author

Darlene R. Stille is a science editor and writer. She has lived in Chicago, Illinois, all her life. When she was in high school, she fell in love with science. While attending the University of Illinois, she discovered that she also enjoyed writing. Today she feels fortunate to have a career that allows her to pursue both her interests. Darlene R. Stille has written more than thirty books for young people.